Music Minus One

3804

EASY JAZZ DUETS

FOR TWO TRUMPETS

T0156374

©2002 MMO Music Group, Inc. All rights reserved.

The Green Danube

♩ = 152 2 bar drum intro.

Easy

Tone Colors

♩ = 88 2 bar drum intro.

Easy

Reaching Up

♩ = 160 2 bar drum intro.

Easy

Uptown-Downtown

♩ = 126 2 bar drum intro.

Easy

Main Street

♩ = 112 2 bar drum intro.

Easy to Medium

Ski Slope

♩ = 108 2 bar drum intro.

Easy to Medium

Doin' Your Chores

♩ = 138 2 bar bass & drum intro.

Easy to Medium

Stop and Go

♩ = 132 2 bar bass & drum intro. (pick-up)

Easy to Medium

Glider

♩ = 92 2 bar bass intro.

Easy

Jumper

♩ = 132 2 bar bass & drum intro.

Easy to Medium

Da   Dit

♩ = 126 2 bar drum intro. (pick-up)

Easy to Medium

Hot Fudge

♩ = 132 2 bar bass & drum intro.

Medium

Tijuana

♩ = 144 2 bar drum intro.

Medium

La De Da De

♩ = 108 1½ bar bass & drum intro.

Medium

Switcharoo

♩ = 144 2 bar bass & drum intro.

Medium to Difficult

Swing Easy

♩ = 116 2 bar bass & drum intro.

Medium to Difficult

Hop Scotch

♩ = 120 2 bar bass intro.

Medium to Difficult

Swingin' In The Rain

♩ = 108 2 bar bass & drum intro. (pick-up)

Medium to Difficult

4/4 Waltz

♩ = 168 2 bar drum intro.

Medium to Difficult

One Note Break

♩ = 176 2 bar drum intro.

Medium to Difficult

Lazy

♩ = 112 2 bar bass intro. (pick-up)

Medium to Difficult

Bits and Pieces

♩ = 152 2 bar drum intro. (pick-up)

Medium to Difficult

MUSIC MINUS ONE
50 Executive Boulevard
Elmsford, New York 10523-1325
800-669-7464 (U.S.)/914-592-1188 (International)

www.musicminusone.com
e-mail: mmogroup@musicminusone.com

Printed in Canada